My Holistic Recovery Workbook

Visit author's website at: www.afrikushart.com

For information about special discounts available for bulk purchases, sales promotion, fund-raising and educational needs, Contact Afrikus Hart at 443-219-7779

Library of Congress Control Number: 2020900273

ISBN: 978-1-7344808-0-1 (print copy)
ISBN: 978-1-7344808-1-8 (ebook)

2020 Afrikus Hart. All rights reserved

Welcome

The purpose of this workbook is to assist you in your journey to recovery. What make this workbook different from others………..it addresses you as a whole person, not only will you address your why, you will also have daily activities to do or write. You will also have daily words of encouragement, daily affirmations, scriptures and/or a daily prayer.

We will also set daily and weekly goals throughout the process. You'll be able to see your growth as well as discover, learn and develop healthier behaviors to dealing with life. This workbook is meant to assist with addiction treatment, recovery, relapse prevention and taper readiness.

Daily Journaling is very therapeutic in that there is no right or wrong thing to say. It can offer you a reflection of your day and anything that may have happened that changes your mood or mindset. It can enlighten you to any adversities you face, how you're feeling or anything that you may have accomplished. It does not have to be all negative or all positive. But it must be honest.

Afrikus Hart, LPN (Licensed Practical Nurse), CDNC (Certified Chemical Dependency Nurse) is a substance abuse nurse at BNJ Health Services, LLC in Baltimore, MD. She has over 11 years of experience in addictions and recovery services.

Afrikus is a certified member of the Maryland Association of Chemical Dependency Nurses. After earning her PN certificate in 2004, Afrikus passed her MD state boards in May 2005.

Her thirst for knowledge and acquiring new skills to better serve her clients has led her to become a certified instructor for: American Heart Association CPR and First Aid, Mental Health First Aid (adult and youth), ServSafe Instructor & Proctor and Phlebotomy. She is also a Reiki Practitioner, Acupuncture Detoxification Specialist and Y12SR Leader for yoga 12 step recovery.

She has volunteered time and funds to several organizations including K.I.S.S. Inc., Total Harmony Enterprises and Sunday Dinner. Afrikus has also volunteered to assist the Baltimore City Fire Department with their candidate screenings.

Afrikus is currently in the process of writing a series of resources and materials surrounding recovery and how wellness can aid in a successful recovery journey.

WEEK ONE

Daily Affirmation

I am the only thing in control of my life.

Daily Scripture

Psalm 46:1-3 God, or the higher power as you see it, is our refuge and strength, an ever-present help in trouble. Therefore we will not fear, though the earth give way and the mountains fall into the heart of the sea, though its waters roar and foam and the mountains quake with their surging.

My Weekly goal:

Name a goal for the week and follow through with its completion.

_____
_____
_____
_____
_____
_____
_____
_____
_____
_____
_____
_____
_____
_____

The Beginning

Why did you start using? You must identify your addiction and how it began because if you don't get to the root of your issues, you're setting yourself up for failure. Acknowledge possible triggers for yourself. You have to work on yourself so you can have inner peace and strength for when you need it and most importantly for when life shows up.

Why did you start using?

_____
_____
_____
_____
_____
_____

Was it in your control? If not, why are you continuing to punish yourself?

_____
_____
_____
_____
_____
_____

When you started using, what emotion did it hide? (what were you trying to dull/drown?)

_____
_____
_____
_____
_____

My Daily Journal: Here you can write down your thoughts and feelings along your journey. What happened today? What am I feeling?

12 Steps of Recovery

1. We admitted that we were powerless over our addiction; that our lives had become unmanageable.

When you see the disasters your addiction has caused and acknowledge your real need for help, you face reality with humility and open the door for a changed life.

Daily Affirmation

I am stronger than temptation.

Daily Scripture

Proverbs 18:10 The name of the Lord is a strong tower; the righteous run into it and are safe.

Triggers

What are your triggers? What happens that would cause you to use? You have to be aware of what causes you to use, so you can come up with an alternative behavior or activity to replace the drug use.

What causes me to use?

_____
_____
_____
_____
_____
_____

How did it make me feel later?

_____
_____
_____
_____
_____
_____
_____
_____

My Daily Journal: Here you can write down your thoughts and feelings along your journey. What happened today? What am I feeling?

12 Steps of Recovery

2. We came to believe that a Power greater than ourselves could restore us to sanity.

You learn that your life can turn from hopeless to hopeful - because there is a stronger Power outside of yourself that is able to piece your life back together and renew you. You have the personal choice to decide what or who that Higher Power is for you.

Daily Affirmation

Every day, in every way, I am getting better.

Daily Scripture

Isaiah 41:10 So do not fear, for I am with you; do not be dismayed, for I am your God, or your higher power as you see it, . I will strengthen you and help you; I will uphold you with my righteous right hand.

Change your environment

Now that you've changed your mentality and mindset, you must change the people you're surrounded by. If the people you used to hang out with are still in an active addiction, you need to let them go. They are comfortable where they are and are ultimately not going to contribute to you gaining your focus or well being. If you continue to hang around those individuals, that increases your chance of a relapse because it'll be readily available to use with little to no consideration for you.

How are you going to deal with family/friends who are still in active addiction?

_____
_____
_____
_____
_____
_____
_____
_____
_____
_____
_____
_____

My Daily Journal: Here you can write down your thoughts and feelings along your journey. What happened today? What am I feeling?

12 Steps of Recovery

3. We made a decision to turn our will and our lives over to the care of God as we understood Him.

Your heart, mind and will take action by surrendering to this Higher Power. You trust that this Higher Power will guide your behaviors with better wisdom and care than you can do by yourself.

Daily Affirmation

I deserve to be sober.

Daily Scripture

Exodus 15:2 The Lord is my strength and my song; he has given me victory. This is my God, or your higher power as you see it, and I will praise him— and I will exalt him!

<u>OLD and NEW</u>

List some old behaviors and or activities you went through with that you knew were wrong. Compare that list to some new behaviors that can be substituted to aid in your recovery

OLD	NEW

My Daily Journal: Here you can write down your thoughts and feelings along your journey. What happened today? What am I feeling?

_____
_____
_____
_____
_____
_____
_____
_____
_____
_____
_____
_____
_____
_____
_____
_____
_____
_____
_____
_____
_____
_____
_____
_____
_____

My Daily Journal:

You will have a weekly scenario so you can learn to apply/implement what you know and have learned to your life. Remember you can know it and be able to recite it front & back but it's useless if you don't apply it when you need it. Only YOU can change the outcome.

Week One Scenario:

When you get the urge to use, what can you do ? What do you have to lose if you use? If you use, would it be worth it?

_____
_____
_____
_____
_____
_____
_____
_____
_____
_____
_____
_____
_____

Weekly Reflection: How did your week go? Did you accomplish your weekly goal you set for yourself? If so, how did you do it? Did you face any new challenges, if so how did you handle it? If you didn't accomplish your goal, what happened & what can you do different next week?

_____
_____
_____
_____
_____
_____
_____
_____
_____
_____
_____
_____
_____
_____
_____
_____
_____
_____
_____
_____
_____
_____
_____
_____
_____
_____

Week Two

Daily affirmation

    I am in control.

Daily Scripture

Psalm 9:9-10 The Lord is a refuge for the oppressed, a stronghold in times of trouble.

My Weekly goal:

Name a goal for the week and follow through with its completion.

_____
_____
_____
_____
_____
_____
_____
_____
_____
_____
_____
_____
_____

Your Motivation

When you start your journey to recovery, what's your why? Why are you getting clean or detoxing? What's going to help you stay clean? If you're doing it for the wrong reasons, you're most likely not going to be successful. What if something happens to that reason that you're deciding to detox or get clean, what's going to ultimately keep you going?

Why are you getting clean or detoxing?

___

What's keeping you going?

___

My Daily Journal: Here you can write down your thoughts and feelings along your journey. What happened today? What am I feeling?

_____
_____
_____
_____
_____
_____
_____
_____
_____
_____
_____
_____
_____
_____
_____
_____
_____
_____
_____
_____
_____
_____
_____

12 Steps of Recovery

4. We made a searching and fearless moral inventory of ourselves.

As you gently try to peel away the many layers of your being and better understand your depths, you allow yourself to experience a much fuller healing, restoration and freedom.

Daily Affirmation:
   I am worthy of great things.

Daily Scripture:
   Psalm 34:10b Those who seek the Lord, (or your higher power as you see it) lack no good thing.

Replacement

When you're in active addiction, you're used to chasing a high or a feeling. This is a great time to consider prior unmet goals or dreams, furthering your education, obtain some type of skills training or certifications. You could also start job training or volunteering at a school or church.

Now that you're changing your life style, what you are you going to do to replace what you were chasing?

_____
_____
_____
_____
_____
_____
_____
_____
_____
_____
_____
_____
_____
_____
_____

My Daily Journal: Here you can write down your thoughts and feelings along your journey. What happened today? What am I feeling?

12 Steps of Recovery

5. We admitted to God, to ourselves, and to another human being the exact nature of our wrongs.

Now that you've more closely examined yourself, you gather your courage and confess - to yourself, to others and to your Higher Power - the darkness that you find inside yourself. By admitting what you've been previously hiding, you can better accept yourself and make changes in your relationships.

Daily Affirmation:

Every day, in every way, I am getting better.

Daily Scripture:

Isaiah 26: 3-4 Those of steadfast mind you keep in peace—because they trust in you. Trust in the Lord forever, for in the Lord God you have an everlasting rock.

Coping Mechanisms

You will have to utilize a variety of coping mechanisms to be successful in your recovery. Earlier we discussed about triggers now we

Some coping strategies you can do when you get stressed are:

Walking

Riding a Bike

Journaling

What are some other things that you can think of to do when you face temptation?

_____
_____
_____
_____
_____
_____
_____
_____
_____
_____

My Daily Journal: Here you can write down your thoughts and feelings along your journey. What happened today? What am I feeling?

_____
_____
_____
_____
_____
_____
_____
_____
_____
_____
_____
_____
_____
_____
_____
_____
_____
_____
_____
_____
_____
_____
_____
_____
_____

12 Steps of Recovery

6. We were entirely ready to have God remove all these defects of character.

By working through your fears and uncertainties about becoming a better person and making the changes you need to make in your life, you prepare yourself to invite your Higher Power to change you.

Daily Affirmation:

    I am worthy of great things.

Daily Scripture:

    1 Chronicles 16:11 Seek the LORD (or your higher power as you see it) and his strength; seek his presence continually!

<u>Self Care, Self Love</u>

Take time to treat yourself to something! You have to take care of you before you can take care of anyone else

What are some things you can do to treat yourself?

_____
_____
_____
_____
_____
_____
_____

What are your best attributes?

_____
_____
_____
_____
_____
_____

My Daily Journal: Here you can write down your thoughts and feelings along your journey. What happened today? What am I feeling?

Week Two Scenario:

One of your friends you used to use with calls you out for thinking you're "better than everyone now that you're out". They want you to prove your loyalty by using with them " just one time". What ar you going to do?

Weekly Reflection: How did your week go? Did you accomplish your weekly goal you set for yourself? If so, how did you do it? Did you face any new challenges, if so, how did you handle it? If you didn't accomplish your goal, what happened & what can you do different next week?

_____
_____
_____
_____
_____
_____
_____
_____
_____
_____
_____
_____
_____
_____
_____
_____
_____
_____
_____
_____
_____
_____
_____

Week Three

Daily affirmation

I like the person I'm becoming.

Daily Scripture

Psalm 32:7-8 You are my hiding place; you will protect me from trouble and surround me with songs of deliverance.

My Weekly goal:

Name a goal for the week and follow through with its completion.

_____

_____

_____

_____

_____

_____

_____

_____

_____

_____

_____

_____

_____

_____

You're Different Now

We've all done things at some point in our lives that we regret and wish we'd never went through with, but we can't change the past. Moving forward, if you can, right a wrong you did to someone if you get a chance.

Do you need to right a wrong?

_____
_____
_____
_____
_____
_____

How are you going to do it?

_____
_____
_____
_____
_____
_____

What would you do differently now if you had the chance to do it all over again?

_____
_____
_____
_____
_____
_____

My Daily Journal: Here you can write down your thoughts and feelings along your journey. What happened today? What am I feeling?

12 Steps of Recovery

7. We humbly asked Him to remove our shortcomings.

As you ask your Higher Power to remove your character flaws, you also take actions that give your Higher Power greater ability to work changes into your life.

Daily Affirmation:

I can and I will.

Daily Scripture:

Exodus 33:14 My presence will go with you, and I will give you rest.

Relax, Relate, Release

Are you stressed out with family, work, friends, children? What do you do to de-stress?

_____
_____
_____
_____
_____
_____
_____
_____
_____

Have you tried exercise/meditation? These methods are great at burning energy, releasing endorphins and raises your mood, promotes relaxation and lowers the chances of insomnia.

Exercise

Yoga

Meditation

Acupuncture

Reiki

My Daily Journal: Here you can write down your thoughts and feelings along your journey. What happened today? What am I feeling?

12 Steps of Recovery

8. We made a list of all persons we had harmed, and became willing to make amends to them all.

Here, you assess all the ways you could have possibly caused harm to others and also to yourself. You then make yourself ready to restore these relationships through both words and actions.

Daily Affirmation:

    I am empowered on my journey to recovery and all my goals.

Daily Scripture:

    John 14:27 Peace I leave with you; my peace I give you. I do not give to you as the world gives. Do not let your hearts be troubled and do not be afraid.

The Mask You Wear

Often times we hide behind a façade of who people think we are or have become. It's easier that way, now it's time to take your mask off so people can see the real you. Not an addict the person behind the addiction who may not have made the best choices at one point in time. We all make mistakes and deal with our troubles differently. You are not your addiction! One usually wear a mask to hide vulnerability or a deficiency. The mask gives you a confidence like no other but you have it inside you without using a drug or something else.

Are you ready to take your mask off?

What are you hiding from? What or who are you pretending to be?

_____

_____

_____

_____

_____

_____

_____

_____

My Daily Journal: Here you can write down your thoughts and feelings along your journey. What happened today? What am I feeling?

12 Steps of Recovery

9. We made direct amends to such people wherever possible, except when to do so would injure them or others.

First, you need to face your fears and expectations in making these amends; you try to forgive anyone who needs your forgiveness and you sensitively evaluate where making amends would do more harm than good. You then take the risk of feeling vulnerable and make amends to these individuals.

Week Three Scenario:

You have the urge to use and have it in your mind that you are going to use, you go out and buy drugs. You have it in your hand, ready to use but you haven't taken the hit (or dink) yet. You start to think that maybe this is not the best idea and that you've come a long way, what can you do NOW? (you haven't gone there yet, there is still hope)

_____
_____
_____
_____
_____
_____
_____
_____
_____
_____
_____
_____
_____
_____

Weekly Reflection: How did your week go? Did you accomplish your weekly goal you set for yourself? If so, how did you do it? Did you face any new challenges, if so, how did you handle it? If you didn't accomplish your goal, what happened & what can you do different next week?

_____
_____
_____
_____
_____
_____
_____
_____
_____
_____
_____
_____
_____
_____
_____
_____
_____
_____
_____
_____
_____
_____

Week Four

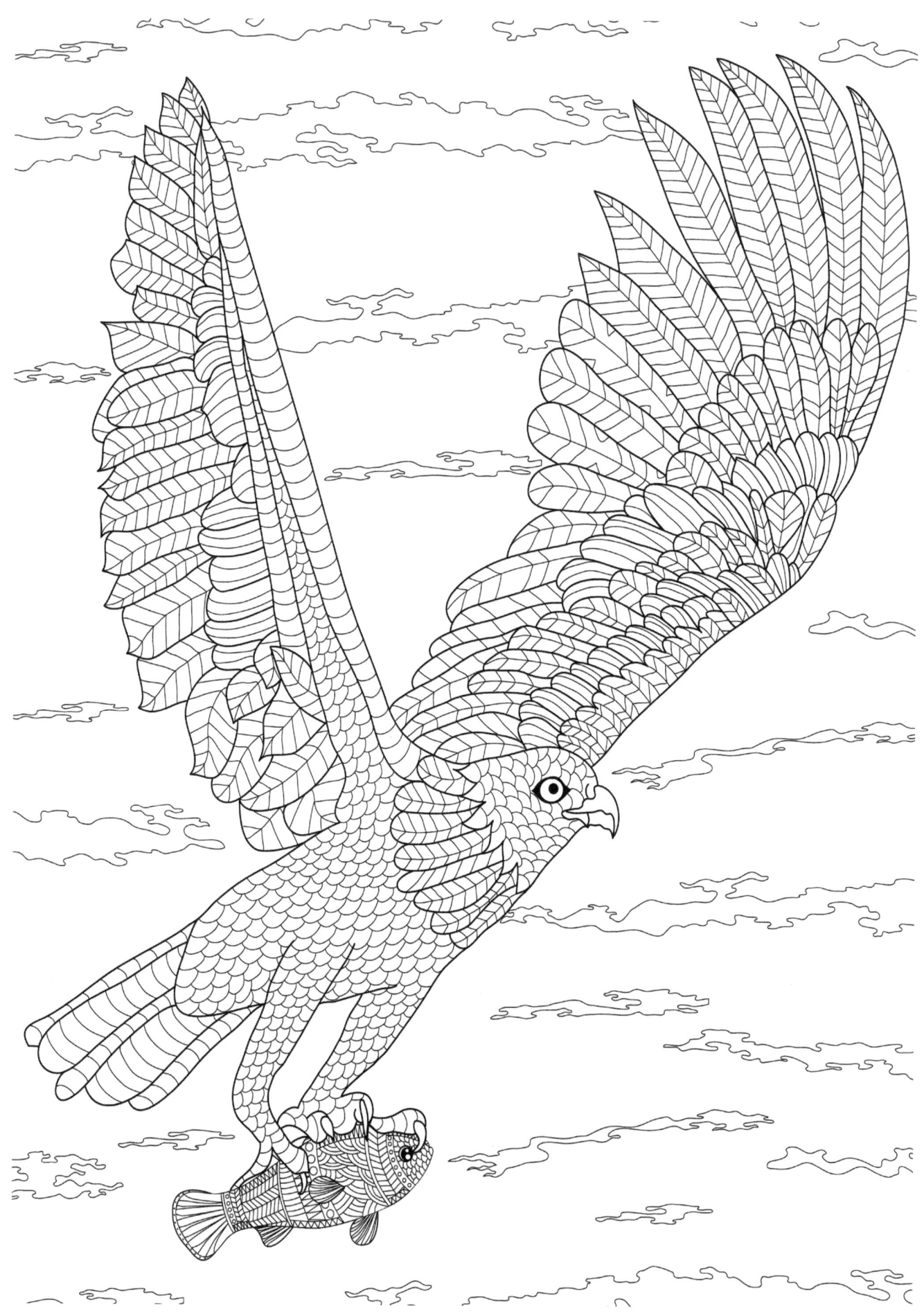

Daily affirmation

I can achieve inner peace and balance

Daily Scripture

Philippians 4:6 Do not worry about anything, but in everything by prayer and supplication with thanksgiving let your requests be made known to God (or your higher power as you see it). And the peace of God (or your higher power as you see it), which surpasses all understanding, will guard your hearts and your minds in Christ Jesus.

My Weekly goal:

Name a goal for the week and follow through with its completion.

_____
_____
_____
_____
_____
_____
_____
_____
_____
_____
_____
_____
_____

Detoxing

No matter what you're detoxing off of (etoh, bup, Xanax, meth. Etc.) do it slowly and take your time. Don't try to rush to become better because if you do you won't be successful. I understand your family or friend may pressure you to hurry up and get off but that doesn't mean rushing will make you well. They may say certain phrases, the main one being "You don't need it" This is the biggest lie. YES you do. You need to do it slow so your body have time to adjust to the changes being made and being without the drug of choice. You must remember that not only are you going through this mentally, but also physically as your body gets used to the changes occurring within your system. Detoxing and recovery will sometimes have a physical discomfort, but they are manageable and a sign that you're going in the right direction. Just remember not to trade one addiction for another, ex pill seeking, that you have to take a pill for some ailment.

If you are on a program, talk to your counselor and provider so you can discuss the best option(s) for you to taper your dose safely. If you try to detox too fast, you are most likely to experience withdrawal symptoms. I would also suggest to do a "blind detox", this is where the nurse does not tell you what your dose is. The mind is a powerful organ. If you don't know what your dose is you are less likely to stress about the number of milligrams you're on. Doing it this way, your dose drops and you don't even realize how good you're doing because you're not focused on the number.

My Daily Journal: Here you can write down your thoughts and feelings along your journey. What happened today? What am I feeling?

12 Steps of Recovery

10. We continued to take personal inventory and when we were wrong promptly admitted it.

You make it a habit to reassess yourself for any future wrongs you may commit as you strive towards better behavior, and you confess your wrongs as soon as you become aware of them.

Daily Affirmation:

    I am more than enough.

Daily Scripture:

    Joshua 1:9 Be strong and courageous; do not be frightened or dismayed, for the Lord your God (or higher power as you see it) is with you wherever you go.

<u>Are You Okay?</u>

Do you have any mental health issues that need to be addressed Do you have any health issues that need to be addressed? Are you taking medication that you feel is not working for you?

_____
_____

Usually during addiction the drugs mask the signs & symptoms and pain on your body and mental health.

When was your last physical exam? _____

For women:

    Papsmear? _____   Mammograms? _____

For Men: Prostate exam? _____

Do you know HIV, Hep B & Hep C status? ____ _____

If you're on medications and you feel they're not working for you, ask your doctor about genesight, it's a DNA test covered by most insurances that test to see what medications work specifically for you. This will aid you in receiving the best care.

Need to make an appt?

Dr._____

Phone #: _____

Location: _____

My Daily Journal: Here you can write down your thoughts and feelings along your journey. What happened today? What am I feeling?

12 Steps of Recovery

11. We sought through prayer and meditation to improve our conscious contact with God as we understood Him, praying only for knowledge of His will for us and the power to carry that out.

In this step, you continue to increase your reliance on your Higher Power as your source of guidance and as your strength to walk according to this guidance.

Daily Affirmation:

I have the courage to let go of control.

Daily Scripture:

2 Corinthians 12:9 My grace is sufficient for you, for my power is made perfect in weakness.

Be Accountable

Don't beat yourself up if you make a mistake. We all make them! During active addiction you make all types of excuses for why you're using, if you make a mistake it's everyone else's fault except yours, that or everyone is out to get you. Now you have to be accountable for your actions and words and if you do something wrong, OWN IT. Admit your faults and deal with it because if you can't own your mistake, that is not growth. You're still stuck in an active addict mindset with placing blame everywhere but where it needs to be on you.

What's your biggest regret, something you let someone else get in trouble for?

_____
_____
_____
_____

Can it be fixed now?

_____
_____
_____
_____

Would it make a difference if you own it now?

_____
_____
_____
_____

My Daily Journal: Here you can write down your thoughts and feelings along your journey. What happened today? What am I feeling?

_____
_____
_____
_____
_____
_____
_____
_____
_____
_____
_____
_____
_____
_____
_____
_____
_____
_____
_____
_____
_____
_____
_____
_____
_____
_____

12 Steps of Recovery

12. Having had a spiritual awakening as the result of these steps, we tried to carry this message to addicts, and to practice these principles in all our affairs.

By this point in the Narcotics Anonymous 12 steps, you have renewed yourself through your unique spiritual pathway, having found genuine hope in being able to stay clean and recover. You aim to both continue this pathway, yourself, and also share your journey and hope with others.

Daily Affirmation:

I am not a burden to others if I ask for support.

Daily Scripture:

Philippians 4: 12-13 I know what it is to be in need, and I know what it is to have plenty. I have learned the secret of being content in any and every situation . . . . I can do everything through him who gives me strength.

Life Support

We all need someone we can go to if we need to talk to get something off our chests. You're going to need a support system, someone you trust that you can talk to if you get the urge to use.

*Who is in your support system?

_____

_____

*Who can you call at anytime?

_____

_____

*Are you open to going to NA, AA, GA? If no, why not?

_____

_____

Do you have a sponsor*?

_____

_____

*Tips for finding a sponsor: a good sponsor is active in service work, have time to sponsor, be sober (more than 3 yrs), have a sponsor, be the same sex, honest & trustworthy and enjoy life.

My Daily Journal: Here you can write down your thoughts and feelings along your journey. What happened today? What am I feeling?

Week Four Scenario:

You go out with some old friends, and they start to drink (or get high). You're having fun, they offer you a drink, you decline the first couple of times then you take a drink (or a hit). That one turns into two ….three THEN you're like what did I just do????? You have the guilt and shame, how do you move forward now?? (Remember a slip is NOT a relapse!!!!!)

_____
_____
_____
_____
_____
_____
_____
_____
_____
_____
_____
_____
_____
_____

Weekly Reflection: How did your week go? Did you accomplish your weekly goal you set for yourself? If so, how did you do it? Did you face any new challenges, if so, how did you handle it? If you didn't accomplish your goal, what happened & what can you do different next week?

_____
_____
_____
_____
_____
_____
_____
_____
_____
_____
_____
_____
_____
_____
_____
_____
_____
_____
_____
_____
_____
_____

MY RELAPSE PREVENTION PLAN

My most high risk triggers (people, places, things, emotions, etc.) are:

1. _____

2. _____

3. _____

Two relapse prevention and coping mechanisms/avoidance strategies I plan to use for my trigger situations:

1. _____

2. _____

Three distractions/positive replacement activities to do instead, when I am tempted to use:

1. _____

2. _____

3. _____

Two trusted people I can call when I am tempted to use:

1. _____

2. _____

My top 3 situations/people/places I need to completely avoid during the first year of my recovery (ex., friends who still use, bars, negative people):

1. _____

2. _____

3. _____

An assertive, but polite, statement(s) I can tell someone who offers me drugs/alcohol so that I can maintain my sobriety:

_____

Resources

**To find a primary care provider, dentist, or mental health provider, call the number on the back of your insurance card.

28 day Residential OR Inpatient Treatment Programs

*BNJ Residential (14 bed **male** unit)	443-759-9556	735 E. 21st Street
*For Hope's Sake (5 bed **female** unit)	410-657-7783	1326 Greenwood
*Mountain Manor	800-446-8833	3800 Frederick Ave
*Tuerk House	410-233-0684	730 Ashburton Ave
*Shoemaker Center	410-876-1990	Sykesville
*Gaudenzia	443-423-1500	4615 Park heights Ave

Dee's Place: 410-276-4035   1212 N. Wolfe Street

FREE day program 9:00 AM to 3:00 PM Monday thru Friday.

*Drug and alcohol treatment   *Housing

*Legal help   *Physical and mental health

*Job training and placement

Libraries:

Free library cards, books by mail, free computer, internet & wireless access, copier/printer & fax services, career centers

One Stop Carrer Center   410-396-7873   2401 Liberty Heights Avenue

Provide a variety of employment and support resources to assist job seekers in achieving their employment goals. Meet with consultants to discuss career exploration, referrals to training programs, résumé preparation, and workshops to enhance job seeking skills and work readiness. Access computers with Internet access, printers, photocopiers, fax machines, telephones, and a variety of job search resource materials. Legal Assistance

South Baltimore Learning Center   410-625-4215   28 E Ostend St # A

Offer GED preparation, adult literacy classes, tutoring, computer literacy classes as well as job readiness.

Baltimore Crisis Response Inc   24Hour hotline 410-433-5175

If you need to detox off of opiates, benzodiazepines and/or alcohol. OR if you are having a mental health crisis.

SAMHSA's National Helpline –   1-800-662-HELP (4357)

confidential, free, 24-hour-a-day, 365-day-a-year, information service, in English and Spanish, for individuals and family members facing mental and/or substance use disorders. This service provides referrals to local treatment facilities, support groups, and community-based organizations. Callers can also order free publications and other information.

Maryland Quit   1-800-QUIT-NOW   https://www.mdquit.org/quitline

Resources to assist those interested to stop smoking

Callers may receive free NRT: nicotine patch, nicotine gum, lozenges, and combination therapy (while supplies last).

ACKNOWLEDGEMENT OF COMPLETION

I, (clinician) _____

have verified and acknowledged that (client) _____

completed the Holistic Recovery Workbook and a Relapse Prevention Plan.

_____   _____
Clinician Signature   Date

_____   _____
Client Signature   Date

www.ingramcontent.com/pod-product-compliance
Lightning Source LLC
Chambersburg PA
CBHW060809090426
42736CB00003B/206